SW

splash

o p q r s t u v w x y z

First published 1984 by
Walker Books Ltd
184-192 Drummond Street
London NW1 3HP

© 1984 John Burningham

First printed 1984
Printed and bound by
L.E.G.O., Vicenza, Italy

British Library Cataloguing in Publication Data
Burningham, John
Slam bang.--(John Burningham's first words)
I. Title II. Series
823'.914 [J] PZ7

ISBN 0-7445-0166-0

slam bang

John Burningham

WALKER BOOKS
LONDON

go

zoom

honk

splutter

slam

squeal

clatter

thump

splatter

skid

smash

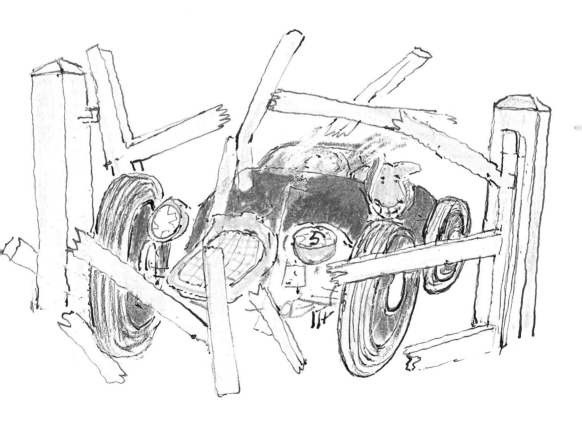

crash

abcdefghijklmn